ARCHITECTURAL TALES

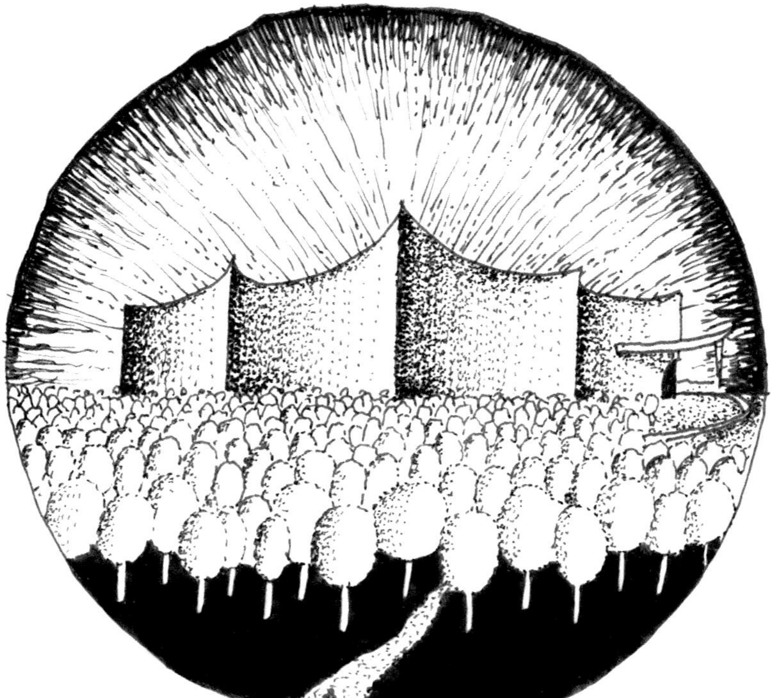

Architectural Tales

Dominic Stevens

Gandon Editions

dedication
TO BE FOR BEE

ARCHITECTURAL TALES
by Dominic Stevens

Published by Gandon Editions Kinsale

© Copyright Dominic Stevens and Gandon Editions, 2024. All rights reserved.

ISBN 978-1-910140-48-2

design	John O'Regan (© Gandon, 2024)
production	Nicola Dearey, Gandon
illustrations	text illustrations by Dominic Stevens
	appendix drawings by Stephen Allen
printing	W&G Baird, Belfast
distribution	Gandon Distribution and its overseas agents

GANDON EDITIONS, Oysterhaven, Kinsale, Co Cork, Ireland
+353 (0)21-477 0830 / <gandoneditions@gmail.com> / www.gandon-editions.com
This is the 424th book on Irish art + architecture produced by Gandon Editions.
For information on the 220+ other Gandon books in print, see our art + architecture catalogues, or visit our website (www.gandon-editions.com).

cover – Pilgrimage Church in Neviges
frontispiece – Berlin Philharmonie, from Tiergarten

The author and publisher gratefully acknowledge
the support of the following towards this publication:
THE ROYAL INSTITUTE OF THE ARCHITECTS OF IRELAND
JFOC ARCHITECTS

RIAI

Contents

INTRODUCTION	6
GERMANY	11
ANHALTER BAHNHOF	12
BERLIN PHILHARMONIE	16
HEILIG-KREUZ-KIRCHE, GELSENKIRCHEN	24
BRICK COUNTRY HOUSE	28
STAIRCASES AND PEOPLE	32
THE ZITADELLE	36
BROTHER KLAUS CHAPEL	38
PILGRIMAGE CHURCH IN NEVIGES	44
ALEXANDERPLATZ – 1990	46
KRAFTWERK KLINGENBERG	50
IN THE FOREST	52
IRELAND	54
I AM A LAND UNKNOWN TO MYSELF	56
MARKET DAY	60
ARDNACRUSHA	62
GENUS LOCI	66
Appendix	69
List of Illustrations / Acknowledgements / Biography	77

ARCHITECTURAL TALES

Introduction

Dear Dominic,

    It has been lovely to correspond with you these last few months since our random meeting, and yes, next time you are over we must meet up properly. You were asking in your last letter about the stories I was beginning to write back in Berlin in the wild '90s. I have great bouts of nostalgia for that time. What a city it was! Yes, I have notebooks full of stories, ideas for stories, and general scrawling. I've never done anything with them, but you will find enclosed here some that I got as far as typing out. At the root of it though has always been buildings. Until college I was alone in the world, and then with clutch pencil, 2B lead and sketch paper I fell in love with form, with how I seemed to be able to invent and manipulate it. This made me understand the world in another way, as something malleable, constantly changeable. Do you remember in UCD we called the thick rolls of sketch paper "skizzen paper"? Why the German word?

    It's funny that I have ended up living all this time in Germany – that is to say, if we really believe Berlin is Germany and not some "side project", as Karl always asserted when drunk in some godforsaken bar like Alt Berliner or Buchhandlung at three in the morning. Do you remember him?

    You were right, this old fashioned letter-writing 'correspondence' is a delight. Needless to say, I look forward to your letters and wonder about any Berlin visit plans that you have?

    Hope you enjoy the tall tales!
Alice

———

Dear Dominic,

You wondered what became of the buildings I designed when we worked together in LS Architects. As those pencil sketches of mine began to be built, disappointment grew. I still find the results, my abandoned babies, apartment buildings on side streets in Freidrichshain and Pankow completed back in the mid '90s. In the flesh they don't seem anything like my drawings, which, I have to admit, already were less than the image I could see in my head. In this I have failed.

Last time that I was walking past that apartment building at Schmollerplatz, I went into the courtyard; a long chat with a guy who lives there ensued. I said that I had been the architect.

He told me that the switch for the bathroom is in the wrong place, that it's hidden behind the door.
He told me his wife left him shortly after moving in.
He told me that he is often lonely within those walls.
He didn't tell me that sometimes, after cursing the switch hidden behind the door, he sits in the evening sun, warmth on his face.
He didn't tell me that he feels blessed that someone, yes, that same someone who misplaced the switch, put a large window just where it was needed, just where the sun arrives in the afternoon.

I have no control over this mesh of stories that take place in the rooms I designed; it is this that overwhelms me. Love, lust, loss, grief, am I somehow responsible? Maybe that's why I stopped.

I'm happy with a story on a page, in my notebook. If I don't create the man, then there is no man. If I don't put him in the same room as the woman, then she will never leave him.

I love buildings but I am no architect; it just involves so much hassle, so many actors. The recession washed in and I fell out of it all. Well, I lost my job. The lazy years. I hooked up with Karl again. Wasted time, wrote more nonsense in my sketch book and continued drawing my fanciful ideas. A few more enclosed here.

You must tell me about Dublin, do you ever see any of our old classmates?

With warm thoughts,
Alice

Dear Dominic,

    Why all the church stories you ask?
Yes, it's an unhealthy addiction for sure. It's not that I believe in all that; I had my fill of nuns and their God in Ireland. My childhood was crowded with them and with Him. No! No! I haven't found the Lord!!! I just love the event of a church; a church is never humdrum. I think we all miss sitting peacefully once a week in a large beautiful chamber, drawing breath, side by side with our neighbours. Some of those brick Expressionist churches in Northern Germany are extraordinary.

    I have always wondered if we were destined to each just have one story, or could we have had others? When Le Corbusier talks grandly of the "architectural promenade", I imagine he sees people progressing on just one prescribed route through a building, but didn't he realise that that's not how we behave? We go where we please. Here and there, willy-nilly. That is why novels almost always disappoint me; we are expected to follow the one line the author sets out. Bumping into you again was not how the grand author set things out. What do you think? Are we way off script?

    Don't skip ahead. Don't read the last page. Yes, I suppose that you can show these stories to your publisher friend. Just don't pass me on the rejection letter!

    Write soon
    Alice

―――――

Dear Dominic,

    I must say, I dropped your letter in fright, I'm not sure how I feel about having these things printed in a book. I just don't like the idea of them being fixed. I still play with them, changing endings, altering settings, editing sentences, until I forget about them and move onto something else. I like to think of other versions of me too, other endings. Printed in a book we will all be stuck, as fixed as a building.

    Waking up and settling down at this page again in the morning sun makes me want to tell you a secret. Writing was the drug that calmed things down. Writing sets it out, doesn't it? When I delve around inside, when I pull these half-formed, barely understood stories from my gut and then try to write them, they crystallise, and these crystals that were once in me exist in respect to the words that I have written. This allows me to leave the past behind, allows me to maybe move forward. I did this for me though, not for public consumption. What happens when memories become words on a page, become stories in a book and then are shared with others?

At some stage during the night I dreamed about reading my stories to you in a beautiful red-hued room. It was very calming and I woke up truly happy.

Yes, I will go for it, let him publish them. If I'm to be Scheherazade, please promise not to kill me.

The rest is history.

Of course.

Alice

Germany

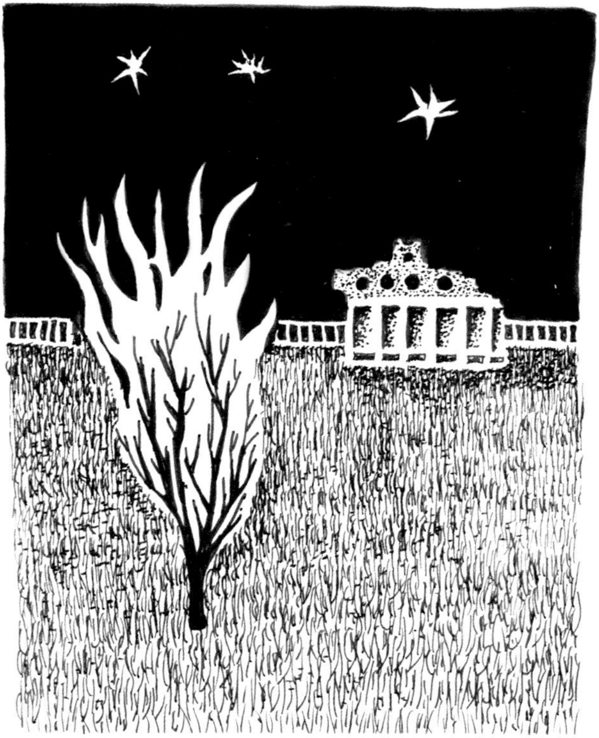

Anhalter Bahnhof
architect – Franz Heinrich Schwechten

I remember one night, blurry, dreamlike.

Do you remember it too? Were you around that night? Maybe in the club? Where can I start, I suppose at the beginning?

We were having fun, dancing in one of those clubs that always seemed to be entered by going down stairs into a basement under a wasteland or down a coal shoot in a back alley. The music was frenetic, probably Stone Roses, Spiral Tribe, perhaps The Happy Mondays. It was probably sweaty, the people, the grimy basement glazed brick walls, the dripping ceiling. Never sit on a couch in these places, they always ooze. I would have been having sporadic panics of how to escape if a fire broke out then forgetting again and doing some spasm of a dance. I know that he was there, tall, languid. English Mikey always seemed to move less than other people, I remember admiring him, I think I ripped his t-shirt, messing, I didn't mean to, it was pretty wrecked already. So was I. Or was that another night? Maybe that was every night? He laughed, he looked cool. We all wore dirty ripped clothes back then, not really a punk thing just the lack of running water in squats taking its toll. I tended to put on what I found around me when I woke up. Leggings, a t-shirt or hoody and a mini dress, or scarf wrapped around my middle. I looked across the bobbing heads on the dance floor, all those rat-tails, the dirty dreads and the unevenly shaved fluorescent paint spattered scabies heads. Someone shouted "Basic innit" during a lull in the music and I thought yeah, that's what's so beautiful. Throbbing, dancing, mental, laughter, we had it all the summer of 1990.

Later we were passing a bottle around, propped up on some boulders above ground, the music, a dull underground thunk thunk thunk.

Exhaling smoke into the cool night air felt good. Mikey looking cool, a few others and then Luca.

Luca. The Italians were less self-conscious than the others, less hard too. They all seemed so sensitive, wistful, more hippyish then the English. His perma-dirty bare feet, voluminous stripy trousers and beard, striding around Mitte like a juggling Jesus Christ risen amongst Berlin crusties. Circus skills, Spanish and Italians, what is it with the circus? The English, the Mutoid Waste crew, were another kettle of fish; didn't they realise the Mad Max films described a dystopian future and not a career path? But they had the best music and ran the best club. Mikey played guitar in a band, that one big matted dread out the back of his shaved head, definitely dodgy but he always smiled at me benevolently. I liked that.

Luca. We had spent the last few days together, went out to swim at the lakes, sat around Auguststrasse in the sun, drinking, listening to all 34 known versions of 'Louie Louie' on a ghetto blaster, arguing if Iggy's was the best or just the rudest.

Luca piped up. He asked if we wanted to do something spectacular that wasn't drugs.

It ended up just three of us and off we went. It seemed to involve walking while Luca repeated "Not far now, not far now."

Mikey was moaning about walking, about leaving the club, about blisters, but then he was wearing army boots, no laces and no socks .

I loved the empty dark streets of those days, I loved that some parts of town seemed abandoned, and that once upon a time, before the war, they were busy twenty-four hours a day, and soon they would be again, once the capitalist death machine had ground into gear and produced shops and offices complete with businessmen and consumers.

I was alert and expectant – what fabulous thing had Luca discovered? A new bar? A hidden Nazi bunker?

He stopped walking up ahead of us and excitedly started to gesticulate , "Here, it's here"

I looked around. Nothing. A parked-up truck, a lost-looking little Trabi and an empty building on one side, and on the other just a fence.

Then we were scaling the fence. Ripping our clothes, Mikey was swearing and laughing.

"Fuckin' 'ell Luca, this had better be fuckin' good."

We started off across the scrubby wasteland. Anhalter Bahnhof. Built 1892 and bombed 1943. The ruined hulk of the portico loomed out of the darkness, and beyond it, he said, were abandoned train tracks and platforms hidden below the scrub. The scrub. That's what was so amazing. He was a botanist, Luca, and had studied in Naples. The gateway to the South, that's how Anhalter Bahnhof was known, and in its heyday 46,000 passengers a day arrived here from Italy, from Greece, from even further south, or so he said.

Here below our feet in the sandy soil, in the dark of Berlin, were Mediterranean plants. We fell to our knees and started to snuffle around like pigs, laughing. Fallen from the pockets of arriving visitors half a century ago were seeds, allowed to germinate and grow, surrounded by a wall in the peace of the Cold War. Bushes of rosemary, of thyme, bay leaves, and beautiful delicate flowers.

Mikey took out his lighter and set fire to a thyme bush. It roared into flame and the pungent smoke wafted around as we danced circles around the fire.

"Fuckin' biblical mate", cackled Mikey.

"Here we go round the burning bush, Here we go round the burning bush," I sang on repeat until it sounded stupid and we fell to the ground laughing.

We lay there together, staring at the stars and dreaming of the Mediterranean Sea lapping on distant shores. I held your hands, one of you each side of me, and at that moment I loved you both.

———

ARCHITECTURAL TALES

Berlin Philharmonie
architect – Hans Scharoun

I got off the S-Bahn at Bellevue. I reckoned I would make my way through the Tiergarten, through the woods; the book said it's the right way to arrive, the most impressive. I'm regretting that now. I tried to dress up for the occasion. I should have worn flats, not heels. The evening is closing in and I'm not really sure which way to go. I thought it would be romantic, but is going anywhere alone romantic? Who would I have invited? I look at my watch. I've been walking for 15 minutes and can't even be half way. I speed up, rushing now, cold through the still wintery trees. I stop for a second, looking around. A fox is standing still, back legs quivering, looking around. I stand quietly, our eyes meet.

    He knows something I don't. His head tilts quizzically. I haven't spoken to anyone in days so the sound of my own voice asking "What do you want?" startles me. He darts away leaving me silent amongst the trees, wondering why I can't remember what it is that I want anymore. That's why I'm going to the concert, because it's not the kind of thing that I have been doing recently. As I walk, so many thoughts start invading my head. I try to dispel them – the worries, the doubts, the judgements caused by recent events – but slowly, as I continue to concentrate on my steps, I become unaware of where I am or even who I am. It's just trees left and right, a path underfoot, and a scuffing of my feet making a rhythm that lulls, left-right, left-right, scuff-scuff, scuff-scuff.

    Now I'm only aware of the muscles in my leg and the feeling of my foot meeting the ground again and again. In this repetition the moment becomes normal. I'm not asking for anything more than this, anything more than now.

I had never heard of the Philharmonic building nor its architect Hans Scharoun in my college years in Dublin. It sits across from Mies van der Rohe's National Gallery. That's the building we studied, with its order, its orthogonal rationalism. Its purity. I had seen the Philharmonic building from outside, and its form made little sense to me, it just seemed too random. The book announced loudly that it is an icon of post-war architecture.

She, what should I call her? My counsellor? I have never called her anything because I never told anyone about her. She told me that I needed to take a step back, to give myself a break. I know work had got to me. Lutz always said if you weren't waking up at 4am you weren't engaged enough in the project. Working late and never taking a day off may have been too much though. Ever since I gave up work I spend an unhealthy amount of time at home, or so Josef told me when he rang last week. I could have asked him to come tonight but then he would get notions, and guys with notions are a pain. I most certainly do not have any notions myself, everything is fine as is. I do make it to the shops of course, if I have to. I have a route, it's just two blocks away. I'm not completely batty. Why am I doing this tonight?

"I'm on a pilgrimage", I say to a statue of a startled looking soldier on horseback.

I move off again, touching tree trunks as I go, remembering someone telling me that in the cold winter after the war all the trees here were cut down for firewood. The trees I touch are about twice my age then, fifty years old, and they feel solid, self-assured. Is that what getting older brings? I can't imagine. Whenever I look at photographs of the desolation of Berlin just after the war I can't imagine that either. All I have is me, now, in a forest, that's all I have.

I stop walking again and I'm not sure if I'm feeling exasperated, scared or lost, but then I look up.

I see the delicate, haphazard mountain form above the trees, a silhouette against the twilight. It glints, golden, enigmatic. My destination.

I emerge from the forest edge and there it is, sparkling, glowing. The metal icicle of a canopy reaches out, people filtering in. I fall awkwardly into line, the glass doors swing and then I am amongst the many, warm. There is a hum, an excited chatter and a clinking of glasses. Too late to leave. I look down to examine my clothes, brushing at them with an awkward gesture, checking shoulders for dandruff as I remove my coat. Cross to see my smart shoes muddy. I had put on my best grown-up clothes. I will do, just about. I look around, take in the scene and I forget to be me again. I suppose that's why I'm here.

Normally crowds terrify me, but here in this place, a part of this multitude, I sense that it seems easier being human. It is a wonderful three-dimensional array of people, a populated landscape, on balconies, perches, leaning on stairs, in groups raising toasts and laughing in unison. I become one with it, swept forward in anticipation. I stand patiently in line to check my coat before the bell rings to usher us all into the auditorium.

You can see the hulk of the concert hall above you at all times, rows of people on stairs and bridges, ambling up into it. I go up and up, a stairs followed by an irregular landing and then another stairs, affording views back down over the landscape of chattering, excited people. The sharp whiteness and glittering metallic nature of this landscape changes to soft oranges and reds as I enter the concert hall. I stand on a ledge, as if on a steep terraced mountain side, a vineyard perhaps. Above, the ceiling is in the form of a delicate tent, almost sky-like, and hovering below it are cloud-like forms.

Somehow the stage doesn't feel so far away,

Central, surrounded.

Somehow the whole thing feels intimate despite its huge size.

The musicians arrive in a line, through the audience, followed by the conductor. A hush sucks the air out of the enormous room and the concert begins.

My mind wanders as the music surges here and there. My eyes close, the stress of anticipation catching up with me. I hardly slept last night knowing that I had to venture this far. I feel my head nodding, neck jerking, resisting, nodding, the music filling up the yawning cavities in the more conscious parts of my brain. I'm swooping with the crescendos of the horn section, travelling up into the sky, floating as searchlights drift around me. All is quiet and the small sharp notes of a plucked violin suddenly give way to the booming of the percussion section. I'm gazing down on wartime Berlin, flames shooting up, the roar of bombs falling.

I'm hovering, looking into the skylight of an architect's studio; a man sits, smoking a pipe, startled by the explosions.

My head jerks, aware again of the concert hall momentarily, and then I'm tumbling.

The lights flicker for a moment in the man's studio and a distant tremor shakes the building.

"The RAF is visiting again", he thinks.

I heard his thoughts. That should feel odd but it doesn't. It doesn't because I'm sitting where he was a moment ago. Pipe smoke entering my lungs, relaxing, and I feel a brush in my hand, paints scattered around the top of a desk. I'm looking out at the world through his eyes, I'm having his thoughts.

The gestures my hand makes are fluid, and the form of a building is emerging on the paper, a liquid shape, glorious. My hand goes back to the palette, a little black paint, I dab it on the paper in tiny gestures. People, little dots, this communicates the scale of this thing, more mountain than building, more and more people are entering the huge edifice, glowing, glorious. It's the curves that I love, curves of freedom, this is a gathering point for the masses, in the round, a collective shape. Not the orthogonal spectacles of Nazi power, all aligned to one thing, to the Führer. This is another kind of society, and I love to sit here in the evenings with it. Maybe if I imagine it, paint it, maybe one day it will exist.

My days, assessing the damage from the raids the night before. Can they stay in a building? Is it in danger of collapse? My pronouncement may render these women, these children homeless, but then is it dangerous for them to stay in this toxic city?

I thank God that Speer has not got to build his fantasies of Nazi ridiculousness, this plan for World City Germania, those classical axis, those enormous formal buildings. I vow never to align things in my buildings. In fact, I don't want to create buildings, I want to create places that feel like a forest clearing, a mountain plateau, places that feel natural, places for the gathering of humankind. Space created not as some geometrical exercise; no, space as an emotional creation.

I think back, remembering those Weimar years. We nearly had it back then. The years after what was then called the Great War, it was tough then for sure, shortages, nothing to build but imagination flourished. My good friend Taut, where can he be now? Still Japan? Like me he had no wish to depart for the United States of capitalism, but neither did he trust the communist utopia that seduced Hannes Meyer and his architectural team. I stayed here, for good or bad. I thought the Nazi madness would pass. I love Germany, stay, resist quietly. Stupid. Evil is around me now, that much has been clear for some time. Bruno Taut. Dear Bruno and his amazing designs for 'The City Crown'. A place of worship, not of a god but the worship of the spirit of mankind. We really believed back then that architecture could herald in a new society, a new way of being together. I still have my paintings from this period too. I stride over to the drawing cabinet and open the bottommost drawer. Led by Bruno, our disparate group 'The Crystal Chain', we nine painted, exploring the future together. Watercolour paintings of buildings at the scale of mountain ranges, buildings of coloured glass and wild alpine shapes. Wilder than I paint now, glowing, heaving crystals. These paintings exchanged manically over the course of a year by mail, each one inspiring the next, together inventing the basis of a new expressionist architecture, the foundation of a new society. A thousand possibilities poured out from our fantasies, buildings to be rooted in the life of the people, crowned in the purity of beyond.

Then, some years later in East Prussia, in the late '20s, feverish dialogue with my Breslau circle, dancers and musicians. Shouting, excited in cafés and bars, excited about form, colour, about movement and sound. I still dream of creating gathering spaces, music at the focal point, no segregation of creators and listeners but rather a community. Somehow this got lost in the crisp white modernity of the Bauhaus, then the bombastic horrors of Nazi classicism. I paint now to remind myself that not all is lost.

Man, music and space come together in the most natural way. More a dance than a building, more a valley than an auditorium. When I paint like this I can feel an optimism for the future.

All is quiet, my eyes open. The concert is over, the spirit of the architect retreats as I look around me, back to the here and now. As I get up to leave I think of this evening, I think of traversing the still icy forest with this destination fixed in my head, of others crossing the city, alighting from trams, stepping out of taxis, people arriving night after night and for an evening becoming a community wrapped up in the beauty of wild, free, enmeshed spaces, heads intoxicated by the orchestra that sits in the centre. The new society those architects dreamt of exists, if just for a few hours each evening.

I push open the door into my little flat. I look around. I start to tidy away the detritus of recent days; do I ever finish any of the innumerable cups of tea? I throw the windows open and lean on the window sill staring out into the night sky.

I don't notice as the cold starts to chill me, as I begin to shiver. I don't notice that for the first time in months I am craving company.

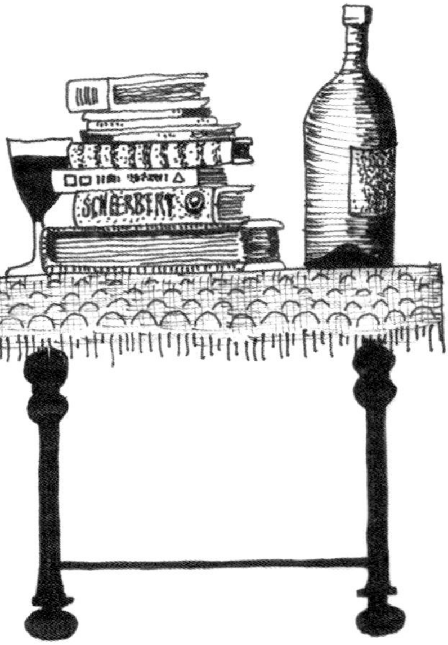
SCHEERBERT

ARCHITECTURAL TALES

Heilig-Kreuz-Kirche, Gelsenkirchen
architect – Josef Franke

The group of men look at me. Sullen, they hold cans of cheap-looking beer, casually enjoying my discomfort at being observed. How can they stand it? The heat, I mean.

Blinking. My eye is stinging as I try to rub the sweat from my forehead. I can't function beyond my constant search for shade and my longing for a cool breeze.

My thoughts are scrambled. Brain matter frying in fatty tissues heated by my burnt skull. I have to think, and to think I need peace, but the heat is everywhere, all around, ceaseless. Now I'm walking, well, half-running trying to keep my grubby bare feet from the scorching, tacky cobble-lock pavement. I hate these pedestrian zones of German towns; shops won't let the likes of me in. It must be cool in the frozen goods section though.

Running, but not knowing to where. It had been days and days like this, and nights. The nights in my tent on the scrubby edge of these towns were the worst, with the sun-tortured ground emitting dead heat.

I know when we had first arrived to look for work it had been curiously peaceful in these rough, misshapen places, these rusted hulks held between three muscular rivers – the Ruhr, the Rhine and the Emscher. These places that survived on memories of their heyday, back when coal and steel were king.

I missed him. Yes, there had been a him; we had been travelling together. Lying awake last night, I tried to picture Karl, tried to conjure him up, tried to feel as if he was lying beside me in the dark. I couldn't because of the sweat dripping off me, because of my hot, airless, shallow breathing. Had he been here when the heatwave had started? I can't recall. I can't recall because I can't focus.

Running, but not knowing to where. I come upon it, in a quiet suburban street. Perhaps I had seen the tower in the distance, hazy in the heat like a mirage; perhaps I hadn't. A step back from the street, yet embedded in a city block I am suddenly confronted with brick and with good dense shadow.

Leaning, body held up by the shaded wall, head lolling against it. A brick, what is that really? Clay formed to the size of a hand; right now it's rough on my cheek, a dusty smell sits in my nostrils. I scan around. This wall is made of thousands of these identical bricks. Each sits quietly in the right place, alone not amounting to much, yet together they create this relentless form. Then comes the steady dance of sun and shade creating a transcendent beauty.

Looking up, I see a tower so tall that it has no end. It reaches for the sky, yet as I stand on the ground beside I know that the bricks at the top, toward heaven, are the very same as those beside me. I can't see them, but I believe it to be true.

Up some steps – there are always steps – I push the heavy door, and the heat is greeted by a cool, fresh gust of church air. Inside, a geometry of simple ribs, coloured light, a textured white interior unimaginable from the hot, dark brick outside which protects it. I sit in the cool quietness and I'm aware of him now. Beside me. Transcendent too.

Natural, curved, light, coloured. This place has nothing to do with the boiled town that I just left. Entering a building can be like falling in love: while you want to experience every angle, touch every surface, some of you wants to understand what's happening, to make sense of the geometry, of the dense light falling on the soft colours as you drift to the place that the creator of this thing intended.

I'm travelling up the intense paths of parabolic forces towards the heavens.

Me, small, alone, yet in this place new possibilities of life open up. I feel a part of something bigger, an intense new reality of colour, light and form.

The architecture of heaven is a secret hidden within a city block. Around a corner on a hot, dusty street.

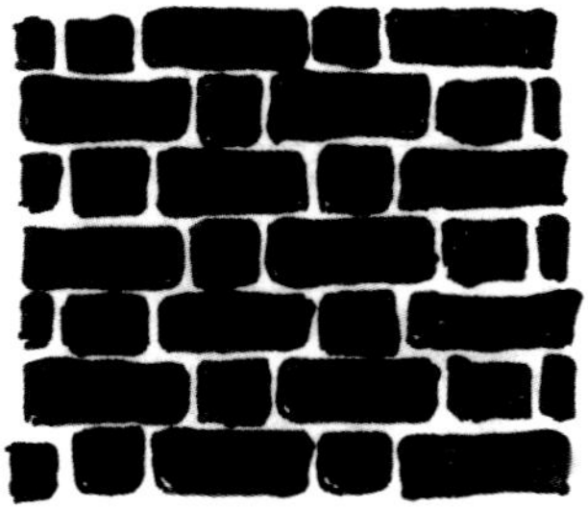

ARCHITECTURAL TALES

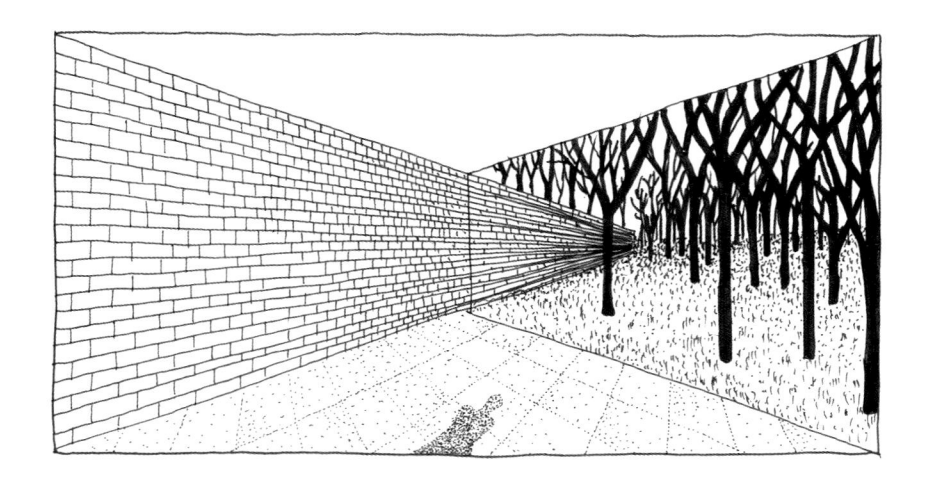

Brick Country House
architect – Mies van der Rohe

"It will be our own four acres of avant-garde paradise," he says, as they drive down the rough track.

She steps off the running board of the Benz 8/20 and scans around her nervously, hearing the sounds of the forest, realising she is inappropriately dressed in her silk dress, fur stole and high-heel shoes.

"We will call it Eden", he says, "the house, it will need a name".

She can't see anywhere to place a house amongst the trees, within this unkempt tangle of bushes.

"We will clear space, cut them down, flatten the ground" is his reply, but she is already back in the car.

The next time as they arrive she is reassured by flat, dusty earth. "They have cleared the site", he says, pointing at the neat pile of lumber. The noise of the steam shovel drowns out the sounds, and she worries about what they have disturbed.

"We have to drain the area of swamp over there and clear a path to the lake," she hears him say to the foreman. She feels happier as the door of the car clunks shut and she sits protected in the canvas cabin.

On the following visit there is a concrete slab beneath her feet and cinder block walls to lean against. Something tangible.

"This'll be the bathroom, onyx like in that hotel in Vienna, you remember the one?"

She likes that from this room she can't see the outside.

"The house will be a celebration of the forest." He repeats how the architect described it. She's wonders if the forest wants to be celebrated.

She styles the house just as the photographer had done, the one that Herr van der Rohe had commissioned.

"It looks like a house in one of those magazines," one of the guests says, the wife an industry associate of his.

"Well, you know, it has been published in *Deutsche Bauzeitung*". He loves to tell people that. Later he says sleepily that everything is perfect. She thinks of the dark forest, a few yards away. She sleeps badly, the trees in the wind tapping the German-manufactured steel-framed floor-to-ceiling windows.

Her thoughts are like the liquid in a centrifuge that he had showed her at the factory. They are driven out, out to the edges, and then they are flung with force amongst the trees. She holds onto the chimney breast like a sailor to the mast in a storm; there is so little here that is static, so little to hold on to.

She feels sure that walls should contain, should protect, and she would like to be contained for she is scared of what she might become if allowed to... if allowed to what? She wonders why this house makes her feel like just another beast of the forest; she wonders why the space of the forest is allowed to freely flow through her house. This house is a horizontal counterpoint to the verticals of the trees she thinks. She thinks about this in musical terms, her time at the Conservatoire in Paris not going to waste.

She paces the house seeking moments when the forest is out of view. Fleeting, momentary, before turning the corner and abruptly once more being part of a perspective that leads out. As the house circles around her, she collapses on the elegant chaise longue, hoping that if she closes her eyes it will all disappear.

Alone in the house while he is at work, she keeps the doors firmly shut.

Running her hand along the marble counter top, she enjoys its smoothness, its flecked pattern. "God is in the detail", Herr van der Rohe had proclaimed to her husband.

She likes to rest on the chaise longue in the afternoons; it was designed especially for the house. "Less is more", he had said to her husband. "It's a valuable piece," her husband's voice says in her head.

There is a thud as a bird hits the floor-to-ceiling glazing. She shifts restlessly as her eyes close, as sleep takes her.

In the deep, dark forest, her tongue plunges
>   into the sweet flesh of a fig and it feels good.
The stickiness dribbles down her chin
>   and is licked off by a passing woman.
She awakes, breathless, relieved to be back on the sofa.
She goes to the bathroom, locks the door behind her and showers.
As she ties the cord of her silk bathrobe
>   she hears him arrive home.

Later, he is snoring beside her as she falls asleep.
The face is close to her, so close that she can't focus
>   but she can feel the warm breath enter her mouth.
The woman's face asks are you happy? Are you happy?
She feels the cold travertine floor under her feet.
Hands turn her and push her towards the wall of glass;
>   she wonders what is out there.

The face is close to her, so close that she can't focus
>   but she can feel the warm tongue enter her mouth.
With the tongue comes knowledge,
>   bodily knowledge that builds in her stomach.
Warm, wet tongues snaking together.
Hands turn her, she knows eyes are looking at her back
>   as she walks towards the glazing.
She slides open the patio door and gazes into the unknown.

She awakes as she hears her husband leave for work.
Getting out of bed she slips off her nightdress.
She slips through the open door and walks into the forest.

During the day the sun tracks across the well-orientated façades.
He calls out for her as he arrives home.
Shaking his head, he closes the open door
>   and pours himself a drink.

———

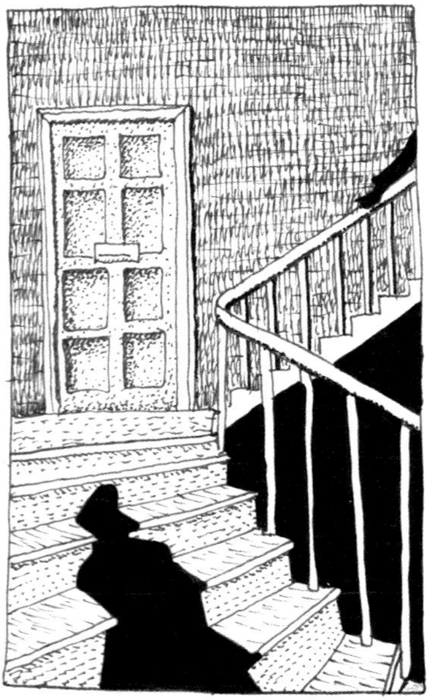

Staircases and People

Berlin, a tenement staircase, probably built in the nineteenth century. Entered from a courtyard through a solid timber door, you go up five steps to the wider landing where postboxes are to be found. Eight postboxes, one for each apartment; there are two apartments on each floor, they share a landing. The overall sense of colour is brown. Paint up to the height of the solid timber balustrade, glossy so it could be washed down each week but it isn't, it's slightly grimy, not quite respectable. The ceiling above has arches, a tired white; out of reach sits a cobweb or two. On the half-landing there is a window; this looks onto a further courtyard. It is divided into panes. Narrow ones to the sides, to the top and bottom, which results in a little square on each corner. There is a rust-coloured floor, and each step has a metal strip to the front to protect it from wearing out. Someone has put a potted plant on the windowsill; you can faintly hear a child singing somewhere.

Hans breathes out slowly, relaxing as the door closes on her anger, breathing in the air of the staircase, which is somehow lighter than that of the apartment. He steadies his shaking hand, balustrade glossy so it can be washed down each week. The supermarket, the chemist, and that appointment, he will be gone for a few hours. He hopes that she will be sleeping on his return. Just as his hand touches the door to the courtyard, it springs open and he jumps; Gabriela does too. Lost in thought as she pulled the handle, now that guy from one of the upper floors is right in front of her. Awkward steps to the side, shuffles. He holds the door for her, smiling; she laughs and warns him that it's starting to drizzle as she fumbles for the key to her postbox to no avail – must be on the hook inside the apartment. Her mother still sends letters, and she likes to get them, but they make her homesick even more than the

Facebook posts of her friends. It will be heating up in Rio at the moment, and here it's about to rain.

Her boyfriend greets her at the door, face ashen-grey. "It's your mother", he says. "She was found dead this morning." She wails and he wonders how they will afford the flight home. He feels her sobbing, and thinks of the hotel kitchen where he will work later on, where that smell of grease will invade his pores. He thinks of the kitchen porter, the one in trouble, the one who says he has a gun. Through her sobs she asks him to check the post and he goes into the hallway. Letterboxes with junk mail neatly stacked on top, he opens theirs – a letter from her mother. He stands still and wonders what to do as a young boy brushes past him: "Do ya like it, my new scooter? Mutti gave it to me." That Brazil guy, what must it be like to live so far from home? He's nice though; they have a cat, came from Brazil with them. Mutti says cats aren't allowed in these flats!

That Danish student from upstairs is passing him. She chats to Mutti sometimes, smiles a lot. He fancies her; she wears perfume. He says "Hi Katrin", and thinks what a lovely name that is and gets a "hej" in reply. Distracted. A shaft of low evening sunlight through the landing window illuminates the dust on each step. She studies ceramics, these brittle things with soft beginnings. They can become so many shapes, an infinite array of possibilities – clay in the hand, squeezing, modelling – but as it emerges from the firing oven, it is a definite form, as if it had always been so. Only the maker understands its past. Our lives are like that, she thinks. With a sudden recall, she remembers the new pot in her bag and being pushed on the tram. She opens it hastily, looks inside and hears herself sigh almost before she sees the broken bowl. She made it for him, this guy with a shock of curly hair, but he hasn't called in days. "Are you ok, *schatz*?" There is the old man, from the flat next to hers, sitting on the bench beside the door, with a look of concern on his face. He heard her sometimes through the wall, laughing with friends, cackling you might say. It always made him smile. "I'm ok, nothing a little glue won't fix." She looks at him and he winks. "There was a young guy looking for you earlier, the curly head, the one with the 'tache. Said his phone was kaput." He gets up, ready for the ascent, grips the handrail, one step at a time, each one an act of trust in his old limbs. The exercise does him good though, that's what his daughter always says. She visits him less now that she met her guy, but he doesn't begrudge her that, not after everything she's gone through. Alice, the Irish architect from the top floor waves theatrically, racing past. "A little hello to Herr Zwick," she exclaims as she walks on up, wondering what words to use to describe the warmth that she sometimes feels on these stairs.

―――

ARCHITECTURAL TALES

The Zitadelle
after a painting by Wenzel Hablik

I'm approaching it and it rises above me. I was travelling along the edge of the ravine, along the alpine lake, along a grassy path, and as I round the corner nothing could have prepared me for what I see. It grows out of the reddish sandstone that it sits on, merging in parts. The base, at least the height of a four-story apartment building, is of arched construction that, though stone, has the elegance of contemporary ferrocement structures. Arches interlock with arches in some sense of structure that seems irrational and ancient, yet there it is, now, new and astonishing. The whole form is rounded, and narrows slightly as it rises with each layer of arches stepping in from that which lies below. My brain says Colosseum, but that's only the base. Where the structure should stop or where the architect should have said "Enough!", a new layer is imposed. A triangulated steel structure with the scale of a girder bridge or a new factory building. Its vertical glazing shimmers in the morning light. This appears to stabilise the building, I say building, but this immense form is more citadel than single building, such is its scale. White chevrons, red triangles and more glazing step backwards and forwards, cutting in from level to level giving the whole a sense of a huge dome. As it reaches the top of the dome, the material dematerialises and becomes glowing crystal that emits an energy, or perhaps a visible life force that creates a smoggy halo and then blends with the dirty ochre sky.

  I have a sense of awe, and perhaps horror, as I get closer and realise that this building that's formed at the scale of a mountain, this ant hill will take me. I can't help moving closer, I'm drawn to the edge that has no single clear door or gate; rather, the people ahead, slowly walking souls, are just absorbed into the mountain citadel to become citizens of a new brightly coloured crystalline future. I follow.

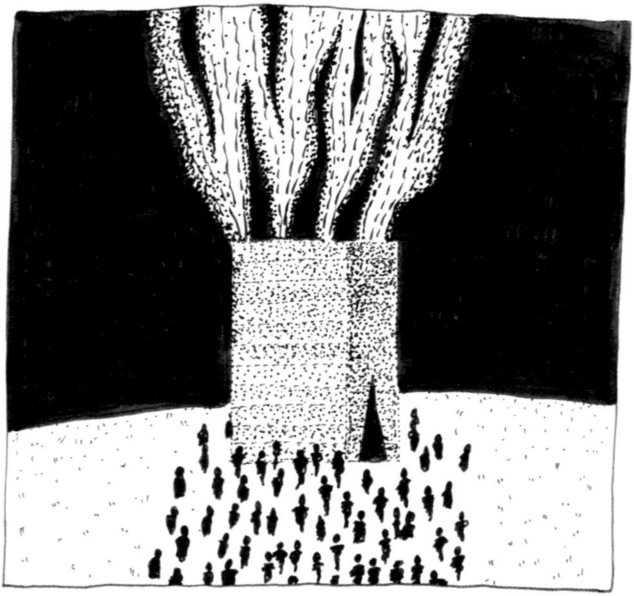

Brother Klaus Chapel
architect – Peter Zumthor

There is a roar of fire from within the earthen structure, flames lick around the top, smoke pluming into night sky. Crackling, then crashes from inside as burnt timbers fall to the ground.

I stand proudly beside Brother Zumthor, my calloused hands rough on my face. I suddenly become aware of everyone else, the whole village, staring, silent, shifting uneasily from foot to foot.

My mind, reaching back, remembering when I first saw the good Brother.

―――

I was only a child, the same ragged clothes as the others, the same dreams of escaping, a drummer boy in some prince's army, an acrobat's assistant in the circus, or just running, clueless, to the city like little dead Franz.

Tall, white-hooded cloak and a stout stick, the road's dust on his legs, a pilgrim and disciple of Brother Klaus. "Trees," he said, "plant a copse of pine trees. Care for them, grow them straight and true. With the love of God." He stayed a while and then was gone, and, we all thought, forgotten.

I remember sitting alone, whittling sticks, thinking of naught while watching Herman Josef worry over the trees, clearing leaves, precisely pruning, removing deadwood. He did it with a calm air, love in his eyes.

And so, the copse of trees grew. We ran through it, long grass on our wet calves. The boys all played together, jostling and fighting. I longed to tell them of how sad I was, how much I missed my father. Boys don't cry, boys don't tell things. Bruises on my arm.

Brother Zumthor returned. I was now a young man, grown lanky and bored. The potatoes were in the ground and the cherries not yet ripe for picking. He had arrived again during the night and bedded down in a stable, as pilgrims do, in the stable of Herman Josef. Times were hard; food was constantly short as famine followed drought, as the weather mediated itself to the roll of the dice rather than to the seasons of God, as it had in times gone by.

Brother Zumthor had piercing eyes, a clipped thin face and a white wiry beard. He spoke quietly in a way that made you feel like he had always been around, yet when he looked at you, you felt him reading you, and when he asked you questions they were the right ones, the ones that made you think. Over the following weeks, Herman Josef and Brother Zumthor could be seen deep in conversation late into the night after walking the hills, woods and fields of the surrounding countryside during the long evenings. A plan was being hatched and debated.

He announced it in our church as we were gathered to pray. Our relationship to God has been severed. If we are to change the course of the weather, if we are to connect again to God through the good Brother Klaus, we must build a chapel in his honour. I thought of Cologne and her hulking black cathedral, I thought of our pilgrimage there, of my fallen father, and wondered how we could build a chapel ? How could we, a small town of peasants, attract the attention of a God that seems to have forgotten us?

Small he said. For two he said. For when two sit together in a place for one, unity emerges and our Lord smiles. Just as Brother Klaus prevented the cantons of Switzerland warring all those years ago, so shall this chapel help bring peace and prosperity.

"How will it look?", we all wanted to asked.

He said, "What it shall be will be discovered within the story of how we make it. Like a parable of Brother Klaus."

"From the womb, Brother Klaus saw a shining star," cried Brother Zumthor.

"As a youth, Brother Klaus saw the tower of God where he would find peace," said Herman Josef.

And then Brother Zumthor told us what seemed to be a riddle.

Trees grown.
An offering made.
Earth protecting a sacrifice.
So shall it be.

It turned out not to be a riddle, because the next morning my mother was shaking me awake.

"Work to do," she said as she turned and left the room. I exhaled, my breath clouding in the cool light that filtered through the timber shutters. My feet on cool floorboards, my wiry arms shivering as I listened to the goings-on downstairs, the cold spurring me on to pull on trousers, tunic, boots.

There were to be twelve men, one from each house. I was in place of my dead father. "Time to be a man," my mother said quietly as she pushed me out the door.

An axe was thrust into my hand and my eyes were dazzled by the rising sun. The world was rigid cold and the ground hard under my feet. We walked in silence, the twelve and the good Brother. Strong village men, a sense of knowing about them, and me, what was I doing with them? I had barely thickened, my voice only newly deepened. We arrived at the copse of trees and got to work. Hard work with an axe but time for pauses as someone else took over. Later that day there were one hundred and twenty slender trunks lying prone on the ground, a pile of haphazardly arranged branches and a bottle of something passed around, burning my insides, my spluttering making the men laugh. I crept off and bedded down for the night, my hands raw and blistered. The sun was up the next morning as we dragged the trunks with ropes around our middles, leaning into the work, grunting and swearing and apologising to Brother Zumthor for the swearing, the dogs running around us wondering what we were doing.

We arrived at the chosen place, a small rise on the edge of an otherwise flat field, Herman Josef's, a good hour's walk from village. A timber church, a rough-hewn thing, is how I saw it given the tools and materials that we had to hand, but no, something else was afoot. A rough frame was lashed together, Brother Zumthor earnestly advising. Next, one of the long trunks was set to lean against it, standing tall like a mast against the sky as it was lashed to the frame with rope. Another was added and then another, all leaning towards one each other like a church steeple. A brave soul on a tall ladder was dispatched to the top with more rope to lash it all tight, and by the end of the day we were standing back admiring our handiwork , this steep pyramid of rough tree trunks and all, like me, wondering, apart from a few hard days work for twelve men, what purpose was being served. Herman Josef and Brother Zumthor seemed to find this amusing, and just said, "More work tomorrow, shovels it will be."

Three of the men had cut the smaller pile of tree trunks into planks, and these were neatly stacked in a cart when we awoke. I ached from the hard work, but sometimes that's a good feeling. I felt proud working alongside these men. Zumthor took time with me, explaining things, encouraging me, arm around me.

We worked long days, Brother Zumthor rushing between the various teams advising, instructing and checking. We were barrowing sticky clay to the site; the good Brother was squeezing it through his hands, telling us to add more water or more clay, and I was one of a team who took great shovels of the mixture and packed it tightly around the tree-trunk structure. Others were using the planks to keep the clay structure square and straight, as if it were being packed into a big box. Twenty-four days and twenty-four even layers, each one carefully measured. In this way a tower of clay rose, encasing the timber spire; after six days it was higher than me, and as it got taller the work of bringing the clay up ladders in buckets became more and more gruelling.

And then, there it was, a huge tower of clay sitting in Herman Josef's field. It had a small triangular opening in the bottom of it. Zumthor asked me to crawl in on my hands and knees, pulling a rope with me. It stank of pine sap and mud inside, and if I strained my neck around I could see a little light at the top where the tree trunks were joined. I took a deep breath; I still didn't understand. The rope jerked twice and a voice told me to pull. On the end of it was a big clump of the brushwood and twigs, loosely tied with cloth. I had been told to arrange this in the centre of the space, and I did this neatly and diligently.

When I emerged, everyone was arriving from the village, tables were being erected on sturdy trestles, food being laid out, music and merrymaking started, and as we feasted and joked the sun slowly fell, enveloping us in grey dusk.

A whisper went around and then everyone started to chant my name. A torch was handed to me. In I went and, as instructed, I set fire to the brushwood, beating a hasty retreat back out through the tunnel into the twilight.

The smoke started to rise out the top, and I realised that what we had made was like an enormous bread oven. The smoke increased and the roaring noise of burning could be heard.

―――――

We sit together here for many hours as the tall pine tree structure burns, as the clay heats up and is fired from the inside to out. Feeling my mother beside me, I turn to her and she tousles my hair , smiling, proud looking. She seems different, slightly distant, and I wonder why she didn't seek me out earlier. My hair and clothes stink of bonfire as we walk back to the village. I have been away for just two weeks, but it feels like an eternity. I lie down to sleep in my bed, wondering, listening to the noises outside my window. They used to scare me but now they make me curious.

I awake at dawn, through the early morning mist I go, leaving the others to sleep. I arrive at the edifice and all is quiet. I crawl in again, and this time the space is larger, the timber reduced to a pile of ash on the ground. I can stand erect in the warm, charred black space illuminated by the light flooding in from above. It's then that I feel him, my father, standing with me silently, looking into my soul for what feels like forever.

"You must go now" he says , and I know that to be true.

Outside, Brother Zumthor stands silently. He hands me a white cloak and together we depart. As I reach the river I look over my shoulder, back towards the tower, and I see my mother standing still, watching us as we go.

―――――

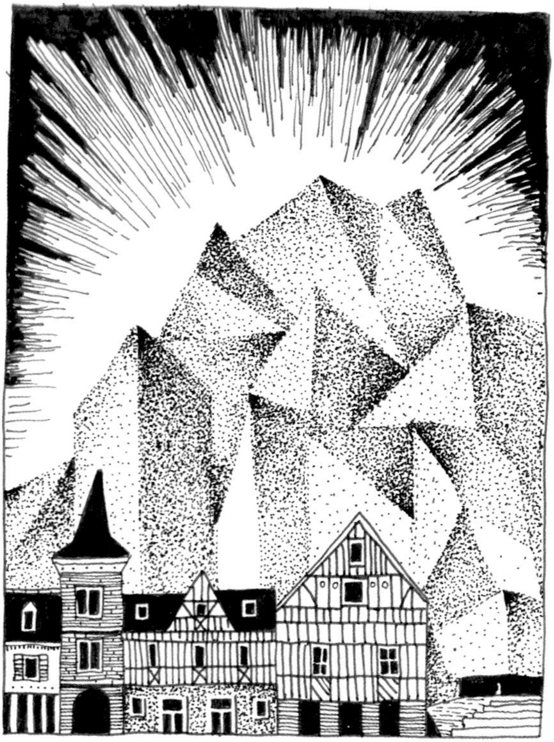

Pilgrimage Church in Neviges
architect – Gottfried Böhm

There was once a town, a small hill town surrounded by the green, the lush. Made of a collection of little houses with steeply pitched roofs and slate hanging on the half-timbered walls. In this town Mary appeared many lifetimes ago and it became a place of pilgrimage. The ultimate goal of the pilgrim is God's city on the hill, and this is what manifested itself here one night while everyone slept. Perhaps the earth shook a little, perhaps the forming mountain rumbled, but no one paid attention. On waking, the townspeople were amazed to see the bare crystalline mountain, and they walked cautiously towards it.

Uphill, above the central square, it glimmered white in the morning sun. An uncanny warmth and mugginess sat in the air. A door, an entrance into darkness, into cool, into damp, into the hill itself, into a huge natural crystal cave whose curious form only became apparent as reverential eyes adapted to the dark. It rose up in the centre into deep blackness where it was impossible to distinguish form; it was high, so high and jagged. No conventional geometry was apparent at first glance, or, indeed, in the following years as experts flocked to study this new apparition that, while solid, concrete and permanent, defied all established understanding of space.

A large hall for collective prayer where one could find oneself alone in the dark, alone with one's troubles and one's beliefs, alone in this huge city of God, yet at one with this hulking mass of darkness and of piercing light striking rough walls hewn by love.

———

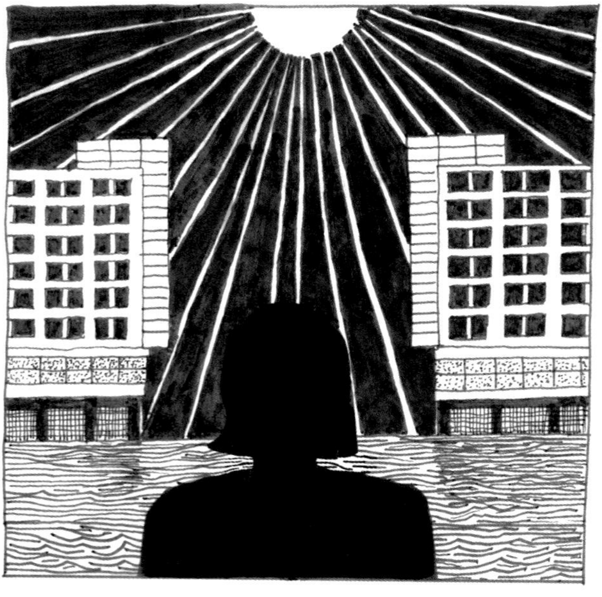

Alexanderplatz – 1990

I'm on Alexanderplatz. Though I'm not sure if I am; I don't know where its edges are. I'm retracing his steps, wanting to see what he saw. It's the middle of the city but feels uncentred. You might ask "Is there a there there?" I can never get a sense of its geography: a platz, a square should be four clear edges, an open space, but this is like a huge harbour with buildings floating around. I suspect each time I turn my back they move, and next time I return, the geography has changed entirely. All I can say is that I'm standing within sight of Alexanderplatz station and I'm lost. It was rebuilt since the Second World War, each building a multi-storey object shouting "look at me" and forgetting to make spaces with its neighbours. I suppose the centre is the TV tower, but it's a point not a space.

    I fix on two buildings.
    They predate the war.
    Alexanderhaus and Berolinahaus.
    Nine-storeys high.
    Dwarfed by their new neighbours.
    Lost.

Above, a rational array of windows, grid-like, and below a glazed band of shops and offices. What is striking is that they each have a white crystalline cut through them as if a huge knife was caught in the act of slicing. I love these buildings. They are a pair and make a space between them. I begin to be transfixed by this space, this gateway, with the elevated train behind it. I begin to focus in and out, dizzy. I close my eyes to settle myself but when I open them I can't see any on the newer buildings.

    I'm back there.

I'm standing on a wide traffic island. It's grass and it's not really meant to be stood on. I'm looking past the elevated railway, beautiful steel, muscular yet elegant. It's whisking people here and there as they float above the city. I look towards Wertheim, a monolith from 1910. It's younger than me and already looks dated, a department store for the world which is considered the best of everything and part of something that defines a centre in this great city. I'm not really looking at these things though. I'm looking in the foreground at Berolinahaus and Alexanderhaus. They are a pair, just completed. They face one another and form a frame. Nine-storeys high, they tower above their neighbours. Above, a rational array of windows, grid-like and below a glazed band of shops and offices. What is striking is they both have a white crystalline slice through them as if a huge knife was caught in the act of slicing. It's thin and vertical and brings my eye up.

The future is here and it's clean and ordered, but I feel out of time. Standing here, the world is rushing past me. On foot, in cars, on trains, it's all a relentless swirl of movement, and this new world is building itself quickly. How long do I stand here? How is time judged by me? I know that I don't want to be a bystander but here I am, alone, looking at a swirl of people.

It's not nice to be standing in public and weeping, but that is what I do. I do this because I feel lost in Alexanderplatz and the only thing that comforts me is the clear space between two buildings built sixty years ago.

———

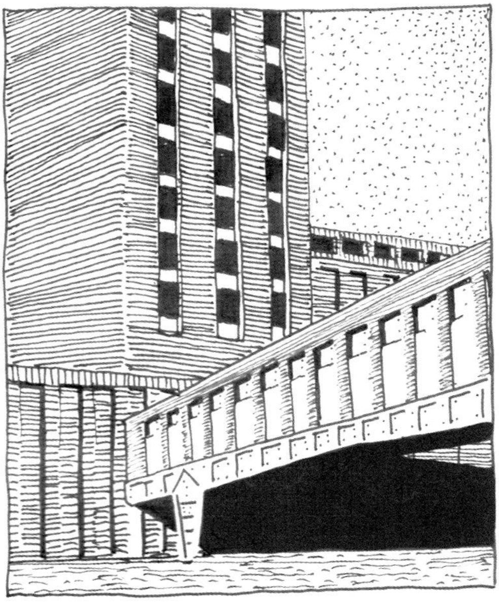

Kraftwerk Klingenberg
architects – Walter Klingenberg and Werner Issel

I had known her back then,

All those years ago.

Even then I think I loved her.

And today?

Well, we meet again on the Hauptstrasse,

She as ever,

Standing there,

Solid,

Majestic,

Athletic.

Oh ! Kraftwerk Klingenberg

Take me in your arms.

―――

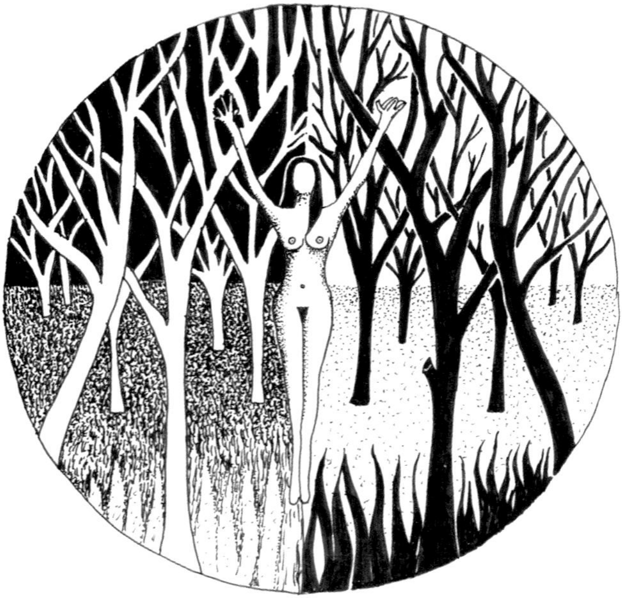

In the Forest

She sways like the surrounding trees,

Bare feet on the forest floor in the early morning dew.

The furtive animals of night retreat and those of the day are yet to show their faces, and it is in this pause, this moment that stands aside from time, that she realises what may lie ahead.

                    The dawn chorus begins.

                        ———

Ireland

Dear Dominic,

    The forest is everywhere, you never know where you will be when you emerge from it.

    What follows are stories of Ireland. They aren't mine, just stories I dreamed, about another, older place. Maybe they track where I came from, track back to the roots of me, the bits inherited, not experienced.

    I don't remember writing them, but they sit in my notebook, questioning me like the stomach ulcer that gnawed at me during those years after the wall fell. I was just at that age, a twenty-something, trying to grow up, just as Berlin seemed to be.

    These stories of Ireland are skins I needed to shed.

Alice

———

ARCHITECTURAL TALES

I am a Land Unknown to Myself

The roof creaks in the dark above me, my heart thumping with each gust. A storm a few years ago ripped up some beams, lifted some thatch. Is this storm worse than that one? Now it's howling. I'm waiting for the bad one, the mother of all gusts, I'm waiting for the rending, screeching sound of timber splitting. I remember fixing the roof down all those years ago with men, men now long dead. I hear myself repeating under my breath in my father's voice, "It's a good roof, a solid job."

I tense myself against the gusts, feeling more roof than man.

Two heavy boughs saved from the sea. A few from fallen trees, victims of other storms, dragged off in the seep of dark before the landlords men claimed them, some reclaimed from the emptied house of dead neighbours. "Good solid timbers," I mutter to myself, there for a lifetime, my lifetime, but who knows, time has its way with even the strongest things, timber, men, whatever it is time will always win the battle. I re-tied the straps only last spring. It has to hold. As the wind drops I finally fall to sleep.

I'm lying here alone. It's quiet now, the wind just a memory as the dawn light leaks through the shutters. I can't remember her not being here. Mam, she is now just a soft depression in a straw mattress; I don't see myself restuffing that anytime soon. She believed that the wind blew away the darkness that she said tormented her soul. When it descended upon her, it's out she would go into the gale and allow the wind to blow around her bare head, her hair writhing like a million angry snakes. Sometimes above the noise of the wind you could hear her howl. You would see her during a storm marching around the godforsaken peninsula, as half the known objects in the world blew around her. Sometimes I wondered if it was her who conjured up the wind. She died screaming as I stood at her bed while the priest gave the last rites. Not three months ago. The wind dropped as she breathed her last breath and I went out to dig the hole.

After the storm I still comb the beach for treasures, and I know this is when I first felt the pull, all those years ago, the desire to leave, to put myself out in the world of these objects that kept being blown back to us. I pictured myself far away, tethered to a tree with a strong rope. If I had gone, I would have made sure never to have been blown back.

When I look out to sea it's the same, the very same as it was when I was young. What weather will blow in? What really is out there? How far away is land? I can think of so many good folk gone, and the bad too. Never for me, I held it together, home, after the da died. God love him. It all went to me, the few fields. A cross to bear. Never spoken about as my brothers prowled away, the songs sung, the sup drank and off down the road, whistling tunes about distant shores, tears not wept, a gritting of teeth, a loss.

I would have given anything to join them.

I focus my eyes, on a clear day, limitless and well beyond that limit, my brothers, out there in the mists. If they still exist? I have strained my eyes across all moods of sea, wondering.

I turn my back on that and look back towards the home place.

My father, he whittled my bones from old branches. Dark winter evenings in front of the fire, sharp steel and bone handle. Mam baked the soft parts of me over the fire, in the pot. It was only a single room then, all of us and the fire to the west gable and the cow to the east. I grew up with her chewing and breathing as I tried to sleep, wrapped up against the cold. We built another room when I was large enough to lift, to carry and to shovel. Starting with the mud, the digging, mixing with the straw and manure. We formed the mud into walls, hands slimy dirty for weeks. Every day since then, as I go out, I touch a youthful hand print on the wall beside the door and know it was mine. We shaped this house around us. I learnt how to form a window, a lintel of a long stone, shutters of woven hazel. Others helped with the roof, the thatch, and as the music from the fiddler died down I slept my first night away from that cow. I'm still here now. Left alone by the old ones and by my departed brothers.

Being sent out, gathering things, moving things around the

world, that was what was inflicted on us, when we weren't messing.

Picking stones, you move enough stones, you line them up and you have a field, pile them up higher and you have a wall, then the field is yours, not the O'Casey's not Seánín's, that's where the talk comes in. My father was good at that bit, in a quiet fashion.

Wooding, that was for the likes of me too back then, and I'm still out there in the dank evenings, armed with a little knife, traipsing along hedgerows cutting decent-sized branches, bundling them together. Put in the fire they become heat to warm the soul. Steam off my wet feet, a comforting smell.

My father could work magic; in his hands one thing became another. I wonder was it the gods or the devils that helped him work his miracles? He looked at the world as an opportunity, his eyes darted here and there, a knife always tucked into his belt.

A chair, given a stout seat the rest is just hedge, that's what he said. The seat lasts for ever, the other bits can be replaced as they break. They break because all weak things break. "Stand tall!" my father would say. The legs become rotten what with the damp earth floor. So every now and again he would cut the legs shorter and then one day you have to pull them out and put new legs in, so it was off to the hedge looking for branches with the right girth, nice and straight. The back spindles, well, they break with messing, tipping, and of course, with the men fighting. It's me that makes the chairs these last years. I like them low, with a broad seat, driftwood is always the best, but Seánín down in the hollow has one from many lives ago, with a seat of oak taken from the bog. Shined up beautiful from generations of arses.

In our hands things get new names. Hedge becomes stick and then becomes leg; in this we defy God that named it all back in the beginning. This house defies God too. The walls of mud and stone, I suppose once they weren't walls at all, they were a field. The field was just ground before we arrived and picked the stones and made it useful. The thatch was straw from the oats. What magic changes the name from oats to roof? I tell you what, the magic of hard work. We take things, move them around and they get a new name.

In this we are gods.

———

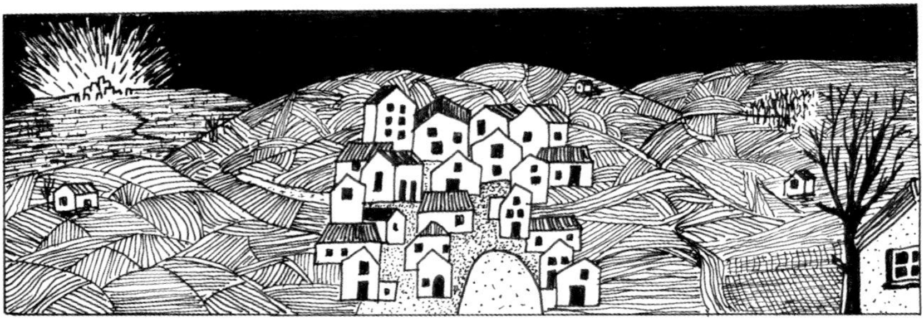

Market Day

Everything happens around the cottage, for us women anyway. Chickens for eggs, the bit of a garden lugging and heaving, digging with my dirty hands around this spot on the earth that is loaned us by God, says the priest, but that's not what the landlord thinks.

Daddy is in the kitchen, no longer warm and smelly; he's cold and dead on the table waiting to be waked, while mammy fusses around Father McDermott and my brothers as if they're the ones that need the looking after. She looked through me earlier like I wasn't there.

Right now it's the eggs I have to collect from the stinking hens, to clean to pack to bring to town. This place is under my finger nails, it's me and the dirt, I dig it I move it I plant in it and it moves me. To tears. It's market day and I will have to sell them to buy a drop of something to be drunk later. To tears.

Town is everything that the home cottage isn't. It's people and clobber, it's clattering, shouting, it's opportunity, not stuck in one place and it's not the same same same. Here you can change eggs into whiskey or into anything else for that matter. Anything, that's market day for you. You can't change how the shopkeepers look down on your dirty self though.

I arrive and I love to feel a part of it. It's me and the multitude, alone yet together, like the nest of ants you find in spring when you start to dig. Heaving, moving, working, all in a big pulsating pile. When many pour into one place, all their stories merge so the story is no longer the cottage on the side of the hill, it's all the cottages, all the people all layered up, all in a big dirty heap. That's market day.

Town is where I change. I change into my best dress, I change my eggs for a ticket. I'm on the train I don't look back, I never will.

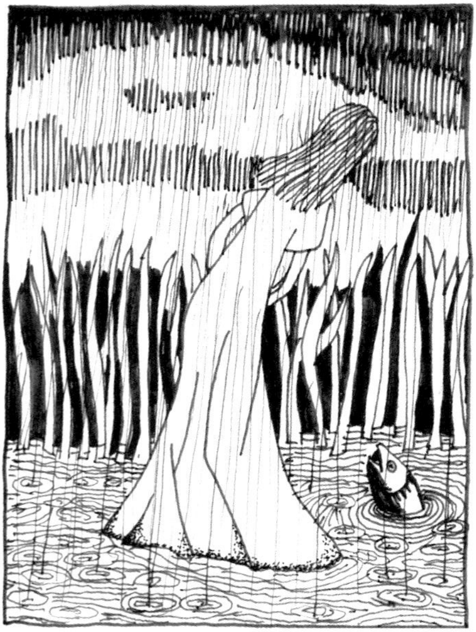

Ardnacrusha
engineers – Siemens-Schuckertwerke

I'm wandering aimlessly as only a young girl can do, through the little hills of Cabhann, great big steps that belie my willowy frame. I'm singing softly to myself, songs passed to me by the old ones, songs of gods, songs of our deeds amongst men. The sun shines through the leaves as I look up, making different shades of green; I love that soft apple green, I love the acidic green of the beech. I look down, and there below me is a little pond; I love how the leaf shadows dance with the sunlight on the water. I breathe in slowly.

    I notice a rowan tree standing above the pool and realise that I have found my way to where Fionn caught that fish one winter many moons ago, the place forbidden to women. I kneel slowly and wait. After three days and three nights the magnificent face of a red spotted salmon pokes out of the water, curious as to my intent. I snatch it with warrior speed, and with one swift motion I bring its head to my face and the hunger within utters to my surprise, "I'm going to boil you on the red hot fire and I'm going to devour you."

    He wriggles free and the water starts to bubble, to churn, flowing angrily around me. The rain starts to fall, big drops drumming on my head, falling like tears down my face, soaking my hair, my dress, the surface of the pool around my feet roughened with falling drops that are coming off me. I'm melting, becoming rain, filling the stream, and then I'm hurtling down in an eager rush. I only know one way, down through the rapids, down the waterfall, past boulders, over gravelly beds, nothing can stop me. I want to be part of the endless grey green churning sea of my grandfather Lír. I will dwell with him, in the bottomless ocean, for an age, my drops changing, salting, dancing with one another as I dance with the seaweed and play with the fishes. That young, eager thing that I was now enjoying the timeless wisdom of ocean, pulling rhythmically to the moon, crashing in waves against the shore, falling to deep still blackness. An age passes and I'm achieving a vaporous state, rising slowly to the heavens, foggy and obscure. I'm a cloud scudding across a blue sky, and then eventually I fall, I fall through the sunlight, shattering its rays into infinite colours. I fall on the dirt; down though the dirt I burrow to find the hidden stream source, and I bubble to the surface again, young, vigorous.

Reborn, not of a mother but of the earth.

The great son of Laughlin found me and said that my grace and strength shall be harnessed as we harnessed the great ancient horses in times gone by, and that light will be created.

"Ninety-thousand-strong is the multitude of horses that shall come when called through the bull horn of progress," he announced to all those who took notice.

He travelled east, over the stormy seas of old Lír to a land of ancient forests and powerful shamans. The one they called Siemans held secrets of magic, of the creation of sunlight from the movement of waters.

From Connemara came a multitude of warriors who battled earth, dug ditches, moved mountains and formed me into a new thing, sending me down arrow straight channels and then through the twisting and turning of large screws before allowing me my final slow and gentle gait towards the tidal sea.

And so it came to pass that through me the homes of the multitude shone bright with enlightenment, and the little farms across the land whirred with the machinery of progress.

———

ARDNACRUSHA

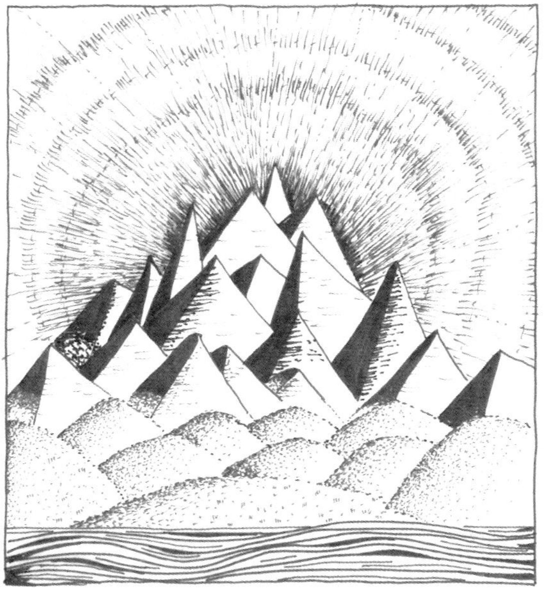

Genus Loci

The long cold time. Eons. Slow, dark and peaceful. My roots were the roots of mountains, firm, ancient and crystallised. I am of the ground, the rock, the cold hard immovable intelligence of stone.

I slumbered as the world warmed up, as new young lives awoke. The stirrings of agile life, the swimming that became fish and the crisp green chlorophyll that waved in the sun. These beings measured another timescale of lives lived and physical bodies wasted.

I have always been in this place as over time its shape changed and I have adapted. At what man might call the beginnings of time they could feel me, some could even see me in this age of dream and learning. I was of them and they of me. They called me Genus Loci, and nurtured me, made sacrifices to me, they worshipped me. As memories dimmed through the centuries they forgot that they were bound to me. Now my ground is just the ground, the rocks within it just rocks. Man has become numerous, man feels powerful and man has forgotten that I exist in this place, he has forgotten the wild place within him.

Man and his hard work. Settling, digging, felling, farming. He seeks to alter me, to bend me to his will, to master me. He is obsessively industrious, and as his numbers swell he creates great structures to live in. Trenches dug, stone blocks on stone blocks, the ground extended upwards manipulated by man's design. They say nature is gone from this place but here I still reside in the things claimed by man. But they forget that the stone was quarried here, the trees felled there, they move things around, is that really creation? This little corner of the earth is mine, or rather, it is me, for I am the spirit of this place.

I like the weight of things, I like the sense of gravity of stone on stone. I don't like the grabbing and the cutting. I put my soul into the trees that drink water, that breathe in and out to keep the world cool. When man chops them they cease to be as happy, for trees are flighty young things as they wave in the wind. Inert, squared off, fixed together they are used to 'construct'. A word of man, like many words it is misleading. Sometimes the trees are diced, mashed, flattened and written upon, the follies' of man written down. "Dominion over the fish of the sea and over the birds of the heavens and over the livestock and over all the earth." Dominion? What is this word? They are of me, they don't own me!

I awake in all my glory and in all my power. That beast within me stirs, their naked bodies lie on the pitted bare earth, the wisps of their forgotten roots seek to grab hold of the stuff that remembers life. A new age begins.

―――

Appendix

ANHALTER BAHNHOF
Berlin
architect – Franz Heinrich Schwechten

Opened in 1880 by both Kaiser Wilhelm I and Chancellor Otto von Bismarck, this lavish and spacious terminus was the largest and most elegant train station in Europe. The roof, a 30m-high steel and glass structure could shelter 40,000 people.

Only a part of the hulking portico remains today, but in its heyday it was a buzzing central station referred to as the 'Gateway to the South', serving southern Germany and further afield to Italy, Slovenia and Greece. At its busiest during the 1930s, trains left the six platforms at Anhalter Bahnhof every five minutes, carrying up to 44,000 people daily – around sixteen million a year.

During World War II, Anhalter Bahnhof was used to deport Jews from Berlin to concentration camps. Fatally damaged by the Allied bombing of 1945, it was permanently closed in 1952 and demolished in 1960. The disused area of platforms and tracks were overgrown by nature, and over the space of forty years it turned into a forgotten, rewilded oasis. Further south, the site of the disused marshalling yard was declared a landscape and nature reserve in 1999, the Natur Park Südgelände.

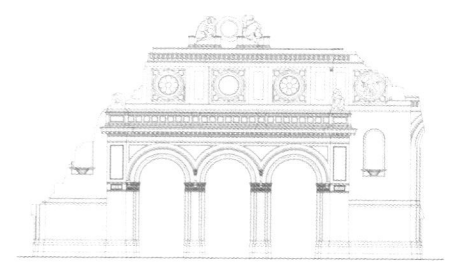

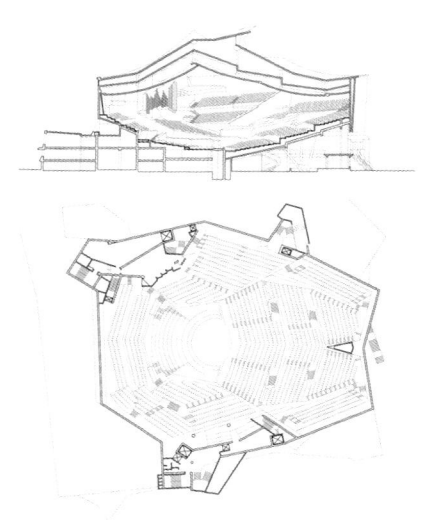

BERLIN PHILHARMONIC
architect – Hans Scharoun

The Berlin Philharmonic was completed in 1963, one of a series of projects in West Berlin's Kulturforum, including the city library (also by Scharoun) and the National Gallery by Mies van der Rohe. While originally situated along the Berlin Wall, slightly peripheral to the then centre of West Berlin, it now lies in the centre of the reunified city, as Scharoun had first envisaged. This later period of Scharoun's work owes much to his time as part of the Crystal Chain, a group that included Bruno Taut and Walter Gropius. The group shared wild drawings of Expressionist, utopian and often glass buildings and mega structures.

It is an extraordinary building to visit. It is a striking almost tent-like asymmetrical golden object wrapping around the pentagon-shaped concert hall. The foyer is a complex landscape of spaces situated between the concert hall and exterior façade The idea that the stage would be at the centre surrounded by seating on all sides became a model for other concert halls like the Sydney Opera House.

HEILIG-KREUZ-KIRCHE
Gelsenkirchen
architect – Josef Franke, 1929

Franke's buildings were exclusively designed in the Brick Expressionist style, characterised by the use of reddish brown brick and its setting to patterns and modelled elements on the façades. This church is on a side street in his native Gelsenkirchen. There is a wonderful contrast between the rough muscular brick exterior and the soft white parabolic forms of the inside. It has been recently refurbished and is now used as a cultural event centre. Brick Expressionist architecture co-existed in the 1920s with the new white abstract architecture of the Bauhaus International Style. These brick buildings in northern Europe were the beginning of a concurrent Expressionist project weaving through 20th-century architecture, a celebration of craftsmanship and the verticality of the neo-Gothic.

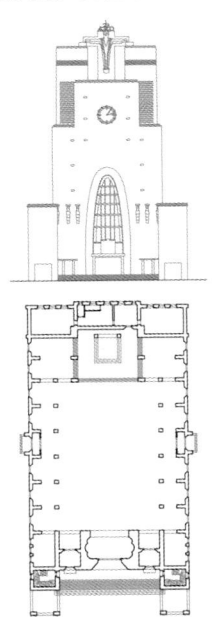

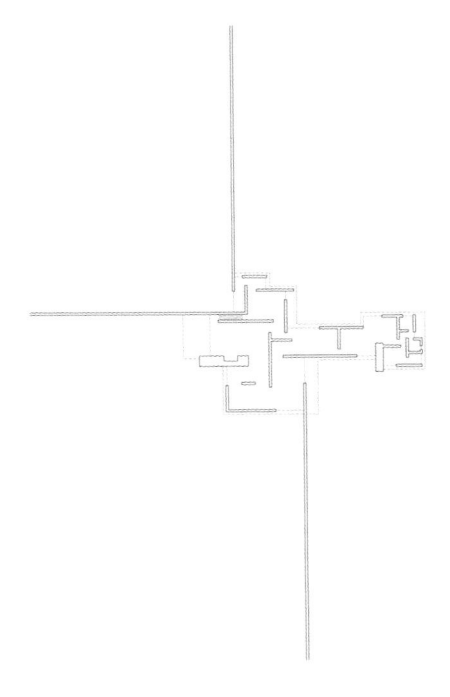

BRICK COUNTRY HOUSE
Neubabelsberg, Potsdam
architect – Mies van der Rohe

Designed in 1923 and never realised, all that remains is a plan drawing and an elevation sketch. The plan clearly learns from the geometric abstraction of the Dutch De Stijl movement, and prefigures his Barcelona Pavilion of 1929. It is a floor plan as manifesto, proposing a new way of living, of spaces flowing into one another, and indeed nature flowing through the building. I have always connected it with the writings of one of Mies' contemporaries in Berlin, the theologian Romano Guardini. "Nature is truly affecting only when it begins to be dwelled in, when culture begins in it."

THE BERLIN MIETSKASERNE
architects – various

Berlin's population quadrupled in under sixty years. In 1850 there were only around 400,000 people; by 1910 there were over two million, the densest city in Europe.

Much of this population was housed in a form of apartment building known as *Mietskaserne*, literally 'rented barracks'. Built by developers, they have a very particular form that was a response to the economic and legislative demands of the day. The block sizes were very large to reduce infrastructural costs to the city, and they were arranged around a series of interconnected courtyards, each the size of the minimum turning circle of the city's fire tender.

This form of five-storey, walk-up apartment building turned out to be very successful – robust and adaptable to changing living habits. Its extreme density helped to create a critical mass of population (twice the number of people per square kilometre than in Dublin), which makes for a vibrant and lived-in city. Each courtyard has four staircases, and each staircase has two apartments per floor. In this way a landing is shared with a neighbour, and a staircase with eight households, a number which means everyone knows who is who, who belongs and who is a visitor.

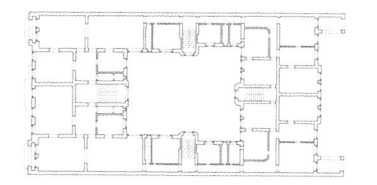

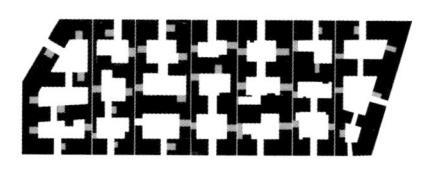

THE ZITADELLE
after a painting by Wenzel Hablik

Wenzel Hablik was an Expressionist painter from Czechoslovakia. He was also part of the Crystal Chain group of German expressionist architects which also included Hans Scharoun, Bruno Taut and Walter Gropius. In the group he shared his visions for a future world of crystalline structures, based on work he made prior to the First World War. Hablik was, from a young age, obsessed with mountains and crystals. He recalled that as a child that he gazed into a crystal, and saw "magical castles and mountains". Growing up he sought out the magic of the Alps, achieving a solo ascent of Mont Blanc while an art student. He later evolved from artist to designer, creating textiles, furniture, jewellery, wallpaper, and combined these physical elements into colourful, refracted interior spaces that feel like being inside the fragmented light of a crystal.

BROTHER KLAUS CHAPEL
architect – Peter Zumthor

In the early 2000s, Hermann-Josef Scheidtweiler, a farmer in southern Germany, decided to build a chapel on his farm to celebrate the life of his wife Trudel. He also wanted to dedicate the site to Brother Klaus, a 15th-century hermit who is the patron saint of Switzerland and of Germany's Catholic Rural Communities Movement. He wrote to Swiss architect Peter Zumthor, whose project for an art gallery in Cologne had come to Scheidtweiler's attention. Bruder Klaus also happened to be a favourite saint of Peter Zumthor's mother, a happy coincidence that likely influenced the architect's decision to accept this unusual project.

The inside of the small chapel is a black cavity left behind by 112 tree trunks burnt out of the cast concrete walls. The tree trunks were first stacked in a curved conical form. Then, 24 layers of concrete were poured into a square frame that surrounded the trunks; when the trunks were burnt the charred freeform interior was revealed.

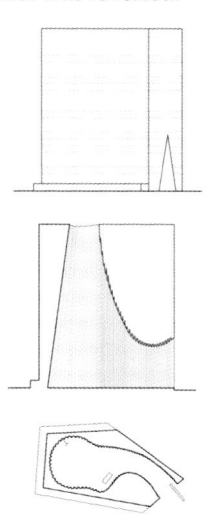

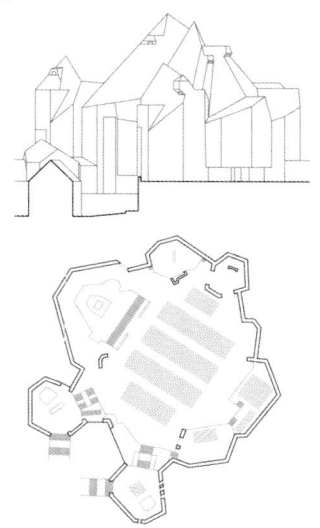

PILGRIMAGE CHURCH IN NEVIGES
architect – Gottfried Böhm

Böhm's first independent work was a Cologne chapel, 'Madonna in the Rubble', built in 1949 on the ruins of a medieval church destroyed in the war.

The Neviges church marks the site of a pilgrimage started in the 17th century by a Prince Bishop to offer thanks for a miraculous cure attributed to an image of Mary. It is the second largest church in Germany.

It is a Brutalist building of hugely complex shape, built on a high point of the town, completed in 1968. Böhm has described his work as connecting the ancient to the modern, and connecting the physical world with a world of ideas. This church does both, a hulking, almost geographical mass of dark, scaleless space that has a gothic sense of mystery, yet is made from that most modern material – concrete. It is a huge single hall that, on closer exploration, is made up of an array of small personal chapels and arcades making manifest a relationship between the communal and personal aspects of religion.

ALEXANDERPLATZ

The plan of Alexanderplatz has altered over the years, as have the buildings that surround it. The lower plan shows the square in the 1930s when it is clearly a city square carved out of a dense system of urban blocks. Alexanderhaus and Berolinahaus (tinted as a reference point on both plans) were designed in 1930 by Peter Behrens. Almost nothing else survived the Second World War along with urban 'improvements' of the 1960s and '70s. In the contemporary plan shown above, the scale of the 'square' is no longer a counterpoint to the scale of spaces in the surrounding district. There is no clarity; everything seems to float.

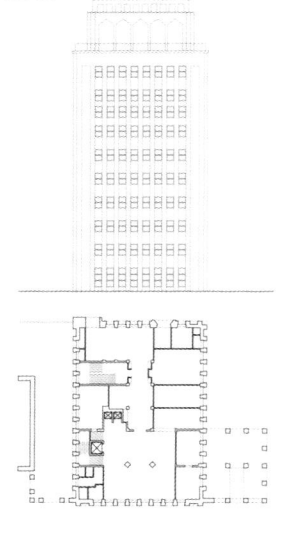

KRAFTWERK KLINGENBERG
architects – Walter Klingenberg, Werner Issel

Kraftwerk Klingenberg generated two-thirds of Berlin's electricity needs when it was completed in 1927, following a concept by engineer Georg Klingenburg. The architects for the project were his brother, Walter Klingenberg, and Werner Issel. It was built of dark clinker bricks in the Expressionist style, and included several administration buildings, the electricity plant, and a heating plant with eight matching brick chimneys. It had its own branch canal with a harbour, and a bridge crossing the public road. It even included an adjacent outdoor public swimming pool which was heated with the warm cooling water from the power plant. It was, at the time, the most modern open-air swimming facility in Berlin.

While the swimming pool is gone, the external appearance and notable interior spaces have been carefully preserved. The plant itself has been technically updated to burn natural gas, and still supplies 300,000 households with electricity and heat.

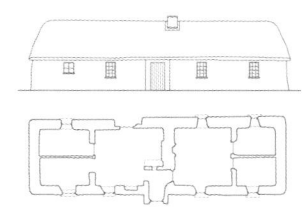

AN IRISH COTTAGE

Everyone has an image of what a vernacular Irish cottage looks like. It has a thatched roof, thick white walls and small windows. What is interesting is not what it looks like, rather how the building is a product of a very different relationship between the creation of a home, the people who live in it, and capital. Vernacular buildings are not designed by an architect; they evolve over time, connecting people and their customs, using available materials in the creation of a home that belongs more to the natural world than an artificial one. It required no great financial outlay just hard work and the help of neighbours. It is a machine for creating an interdependent community in harmony with nature.

MARKET TOWNS

These days we think of rural Ireland as being very car-dependent as people drive hither and thither to schools, shops and restaurants. It never used to be like this; in earlier times the world travelled to them. Most rural homes were within walking distance of a market town, possibly a long walk, but you only made the journey once a week. Market day was the day the world arrived. This mobile infrastructure was sustainable and exciting, with things to be bought and sold, friends to catch up with, songs to be sung and drink to be drunk. If the town had a train station, it was also a portal to another life.

ARDNACRUSHA POWER PLANT
engineers – Siemens-Schuckertwerke

The young Irish engineer Thomas McLaughlin joined the German electrical engineering company Siemens-Schuckert in Berlin in 1922. Having studied their projects in Germany, he proposed to the new Irish government the 'Shannon scheme', the world's first national electricity system. Siemens designed and built the Ardnacrusha dam and hydroelectric power station in 1925-29 under contract to the new Irish state. It was a hugely important project for a young state, costing a fifth of the state's annual revenue. However it was able to supply well in excess of the country's then electricity needs.

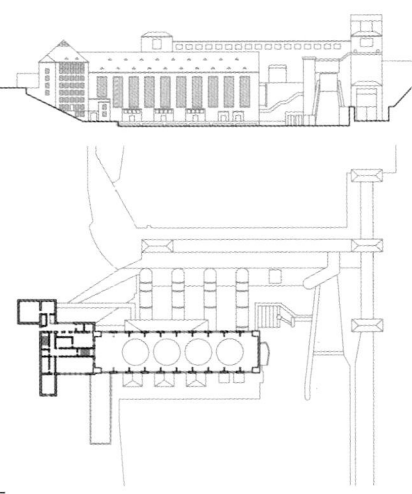

List of Illustrations

		appendix	
Pilgrimage Church in Neviges	cover		
Berlin Philharmonie, from Tiergarten	2		
Old-fashioned letter-writing	6		
Why all the churches?	11		
Anhalter Bahnhof, Berlin	12	elevation	70
Berlin Philharmonie, interior	16	plan, section	70
Stack bond	23		
Heilig-Kreuz-Kirche, Gelsenkirchen	24	plan, elevation	71
Flemish bond	27		
Brick Country House, Neubabelsberg, Potsdam	28	plan	71
On the stairs	32		
The Zitadelle, *after a painting by Wenzel Hablik*	36	engraving	72
Brother Klaus Chapel, Mechernich	38	plan, section, elevation	73
Pilgrimage Church in Neviges	44	plan, elevation	73
Alexanderplatz, Berlin – 1990	46	figure-grounds	74
TV Tower, Alexanderplatz	49		
Kraftwerk Klingenberg, Berlin	50	plan, elevation	74
In the forest	52		
The forest is everywhere	54		
I am a land unknown to myself	56	an Irish cottage	75
Market day	60	a market town	75
Ardnacrusha 1	62	plan, elevation	75
Ardnacrusha 2 (River Shannon)	65		
Genus loci	66		
In the end we will sit together	69		

AUTHOR'S ACKNOWLEDGEMENTS

Thanks to John O'Regan of Gandon Editions for his early enthusiasm and later care and patience. To my ever-supportive writing group – Libby, Cassie, Fintan, Jean, Fionnuala, Julian, Aisling and Jennifer. To David Butler for putting me on the writing group road and for his fantastic editing and encouragement. To Michael Hayes for publishing earlier versions of some of these stories in *Architecture Ireland*, and to the Venice Biennale *Free Market* team for commissioning my first-ever story 'Market Day'. And especially to Bee for constant support and happinesses.

AUTHOR'S BIOGRAPHY

Dominic established Dominic Stevens Architects in 1995 and has won numerous architectural awards, including AAI Awards for the Mimetic House and for Doolin Coastguard Station. He was awarded the Kevin Kieran Award by the Arts Council and the OPW. His work has been published worldwide and has been included in a number of Venice Architectural Biennales. He is a director of JFOC Architects since 2018, recently winning the RIAI Town Centre Competition for housing in Roscrea. Dominic was a member of the Steering Committee for the first Government Policy on Architecture and he lectures in the School of Architecture in TU Dublin.

He has always loved to write, often about architecture. His two creative non-fiction books *Domestic* (1999) and *Rural* (2007) were personal responses to places that he found himself. His short story 'Dream of a Lost Friend' was published in *The Winter Papers* (volume 6, 2020), and 'On the Stairs' was an *Irish Independent* 'New Irish Writing' short story winner in 2024. His novel, *The Coloured Room*, was selected for the Irish Writers Centre 'Novel Fair 2024'. He has been a contributor to *Architecture Ireland* for many years.

Sarah Lappin in *The Full Irish – New Architecture in Ireland* (2009) wrote: "His thinking about his practice is careful, but simultaneously rational and unusual. This alternative take on both formal decisions and his practice of architecture results in ideas that may very well have some of the strongest resonance for a new, reconfigured Ireland."

Alice announced herself one Saturday morning in 2018 while Dominic was daydreaming and writing, something he does as often as possible. A paragraph appeared on his laptop screen, and became the opening lines to a novel, *The Coloured Room*.

"I stop, I'm standing on sandy ground squinting into the low autumn sun, staring at tourists staring at the Wall. They stare back. They chatter and take photographs of eachother, pointing at bits of graffiti scrawled on it. I keep it up and they look at me worriedly. Worried by a 25-year-old Irish woman. I don't know why I shout 'fuck off' at them but I do."

She appears to have studied alongside Dominic in University College Dublin, departing for Berlin at about the same time as him. According to her, she has remained there ever since, though exact details of her later life remain unclear.

Ich hab' noch einen koffer in Berlin (song by Marlene Dietrich)